D0971292

Bedtime Stories for Dogs

Bedtime Stories for Dogs

By
Leigh Anne Jasheway

Andrews and McMeel
A Universal Press Syndicate Company
Kansas City

Library of Congress Cataloging-in-Publication Data
Jasheway, Leigh Anne.
   Bedtime stories for dogs / by Leigh Anne Jasheway.
     p.   cm.
   ISBN 0-8362-2199-0 (hd)
   1. Dogs—Literary collections.   2. Nursery rhymes—Adaptations.
   3. Fairy tales—Adaptations.   I. Title.
PS3560.A647B4   96-24633
813'.54—dc20   CIP

Book Design by Top Dog Design

—— **ATTENTION: SCHOOLS AND BUSINESSES** ——

Andrews and McMeel books are available at quantity discounts with bulk purchase for educational, business, or sales promotional use. For information, please write to: Special Sales Department, Andrews and McMeel, 4520 Main Street, Kansas City, Missouri 64111.

Contents

Introduction   1

Stories

The Three Little Pugs   5

Hans and Greta   *11*

Jackie and the Beanpole   19

Goldilocks and the Three Cats   29

Red, Riding to the Dog Show   37

Snow White and the Seven Chihuahuas   45

CinderDane   59

Princess and Peabody   69

Nursery Rhymes

Peter, Peter   *80*

Little Miss Muffin   *80*

Jack and Jill   *81*

Humpty Dumpty   *81*

Three Small Dogs   82

Hickory Dickory Dog   82

Angel Dogs   *83*

*I*ntroduction

If you're reading this book, you are undoubtedly the proud parent of dog children. It's not that you treat your dogs like children—they are your children, just as much as any human youngsters who may or may not live in your house, ruin your furniture, and run up your food bill.

And, as parents of dog children, you're probably pretty fed up with the way your kids are discriminated against— they can't eat in restaurants, aren't allowed in the grocery store, can't even sit quietly and watch a movie. For me, the worst was when I realized there were no bedtime stories for my babies. I was outraged! We all know how important reading is to kids. How can I expect my babies to grow up and get a job when all they have for entertainment are reruns of *Scooby Doo*?

As I was writing this book, I kept several things in mind. Like the fact that dogs:

Prefer things short and simple (their life is complicated enough)

Like happy endings

Prefer stories that involve food

Are really smart and enjoy stories that require them to exercise their superior intellect

Have excellent senses of humor

Like things that smell really awful.

Well, except for the latter, I have tried to make sure that *Bedtime Stories for Dogs* meets these criteria. Every one of these stories was proofed (and woofed) by my two eleven-year-old wiener dogs. If they didn't give a story two paws up and two tails wagging, it was back to the drawing board.

Bedtime Stories for Dogs **is for you if:**

Your dog occasionally allows you to sleep in the bed (but only if you don't hog the covers!)

Your dog has control of the remote (and flips through watching dog-food commercials)

Your last vacation was a tour of great fire hydrants of Europe

Your dog has his/her own wardrobe that rivals anything you have in the closet (and the jewelry, oh, the jewelry!)

You carry your dog when he/she gets winded

You don't even notice the dog hairs in your food

Your dog has health and life insurance policies (Mutual of Ken-L-Ration)

You fill the toilet bowl with mineral water

You have a special shelf in the bathroom for doggie toiletries (shampoo, toothpaste, bath oil, feminine hygiene products . . .)

So, sit back and relax. Get a bowl of water and some Milk Bones. And enjoy!

The Three Little Pugs

Once upon a time there were three little Pugs named Herman, Ira, and Stan.

Their mother thought they were beautiful. But all the dogs at obedience school taunted them. "Here come the Puglies," they'd bark. Even the Chihuahuas made fun of them!

All the taunting made the three little Pugs very sad. And there's nothing sadder looking than a sad Pug face. Oy.

One day, Mother Pug had to go to the beauty parlor to get her nails clipped. Since Herman, Ira, and Stan were big boys, Mother Pug decided it would be okay to let them play outside until she got back. Big mistake.

It was a nice warm day. The three little Pugs got hot playing "Mark the Hydrant" and decided to take off their dog collars. They were naked and free. This made the three little Pugs very happy.

But their happiness didn't last long. Donny the Doberman—the biggest bully in the neighborhood —came by. Not only did he cover their scents on the hydrant, he ran off barking, "I'm going to tell

Dastardly Dogcatcher you're playing in the street without your dog tags!"

And wouldn't you know, before the Pugs had a chance to get their collars back on, Dastardly Dogcatcher showed up! The Pugs could hear dogs barking from the back of his dog-catching van. Dogs whose only crime had been roaming free, enjoying the beautiful spring day were now going up the river.

Herman was so scared, he made a puddle on the sidewalk. When Dastardly Dogcatcher tried to catch him in his net, Herman ran and hid under a big pile of leaves. Herman was not the brightest Pug.

Dastardly yelled, "Get out of that pile of leaves, you Pugly, or I'll huff and I'll puff and I'll blow them away." Herman shook in fear, but he didn't come out. So Dastardly Dogcatcher took a very deep breath and he huffed and he puffed and he blew the leaves away. And then he put Herman in the back of the van with the other innocent dogs.

Ira was so scared he could have plotzed. He ran and hid in some tall grass. Dastardly Dogcatcher saw the grass moving and yelled, "I know you're in there, you Pugly. Come out or I'll huff and I'll puff and I'll blow that grass away." Ira was very scared, but he did not come out. So Dastardly Dogcatcher took a very deep breath and he huffed and he puffed and he blew the grass away. And then he put Ira in the back of his van with Herman and the other innocent dogs.

Stan, on the other hand, was a very smart dog. He took one look at the situation and hightailed it to a nearby deli and bolted the door shut. Dastardly Dogcatcher could see him through the window, right below the sign that said, KOSHER MEATS. He yelled, "Come out of that deli, you Pugly, or I'll huff and I'll puff and I'll blow it away!"

Stan was amused by the guy's chutzpah. Dastardly Dogcatcher took a very, very deep breath and he huffed and he puffed as hard as he could, and the deli—being made of concrete, steel, and glass—just stood there. Dastardly Dogcatcher huffed and puffed so hard that he actually passed out right there on the sidewalk.

Stan grabbed some corned beef and then he unlocked the front door and ran to the van. He let Herman and Ira and the other poor dogs out. And being not only bright, but caring, too, Stan ran back into the deli and dialed 911 to make sure Dastardly Dogcatcher hadn't had a heart attack. After all, reasoned Stan, he was just doing his job.

The Pugs and the other innocent dogs who were now free went to Herman, Stan, and Ira's house. As they sat around sharing Stan's corned beef, they agreed never to play outside without their collars again! And no one ever made fun of the three little Pugs again!

Hans
and
Greta

Hans and Greta were two of the most beautiful Dachshunds the world had ever known, and that's saying a lot. Hans, the boy dog, was as red as a summer sunset. And Greta, his sister, was the color of black velvet.

They lived with their parents in a lovely house. Their address was 1 Wiener Dog Lane. Their house had all the things Dachshunds could ever want—a white picket fence, big front porch, and windows all the way to the floor so Hans and Greta could see everything going on outside and bark. They were excellent barkers.

One day, Hans decided he wanted to go for a stroll in the woods nearby. Greta was nervous about going so far away from home, but Hans goaded her into going along by calling her a "wimpy wiener." She just hated that. So she agreed. But, just to be on the safe side, she put on her reflective collar and packed a bag full of Milk Bones.

As they traveled along, smelling all the good smells on the rocks and trees and bushes, Greta scattered Milk Bone crumbs behind her. "This way," she thought, "we can always find our way home."

Hans, who was always hungry, saw the Milk Bone crumbs and decided to eat them in between sniffing trees and scent-marking rocks. "No problem," he said to himself, "I can find my way home from anywhere." He was pretty proud of himself.

Soon, it started to get dark. Greta was scared and said they should turn around and head for home. Hans didn't want to admit that he was scared of the dark, so he nonchalantly agreed, "If you are too scared to go on, I guess we'll have to go back home."

Greta searched the ground for the Milk Bone crumbs she'd been scattering. Not seeing any, she looked at Hans suspiciously and asked, "What did you do with the crumbs?"

"Crumbs, what crumbs?" he mumbled as he continued to munch.

"Oh, don't give me that, I can see them sticking to your snout. Now how are we going to make it home?"

Hans reassured her that she was in good paws and that he would find the way home. They started walking. It was getting darker and darker and they were still lost in the woods.

Soon a little boy rode by on his bike.

"Let's ask him which way home is," Greta said excitedly.

"Oh, he won't know anything," replied Hans cockily. "And, really, I know exactly where we are."

The boy rode off.

It was clear to Greta that they were lost and getting loster, but when Hans got it in his mind that he was right, there was just no talking to him.

Hans spotted a light in the woods. "Look," he said, "a light. Let's go in and get some food before we head home."

Greta was nervous about asking for food from strangers, but she figured that while Hans was stuffing his face, she could secretly find out how to get home.

Hans and Greta stood at the front door and whined and scratched. A tall woman in a blue uniform answered. Oh, no! It was the mail carrier! The enemy of dogs everywhere!

Greta tried to bolt into the woods, while Hans barked viciously, his hind end shaking so hard he almost fell off the porch.

"My, my, what cute little wiener dogs," said the mail carrier. "Won't you come in? I was just sitting down to dinner. Would you like some macaroni and cheese?"

Well, that got Hans's attention. He just loved macaroni and cheese. He stopped barking right away and followed the mail carrier inside. Greta knew she couldn't leave Hans behind, despite the fact that his macho attitude and gluttinous appetite would probably get them in really big trouble. So she went inside too.

Hans ate a huge bowlful of macaroni and cheese while Greta sat in the corner and watched everything suspiciously. A tiny pool of drool on the floor gave away the fact that she was hungry too.

After she finished eating, the mail carrier got up.

She put on her hat. Hans and Greta ran for the door, but it was locked.

"Would you like me to take you home?" asked the mail carrier.

Greta was pretty sure this was just a trick of some kind, but at least they would have a better chance of escaping if they were outside. But, before they knew what was happening, the mail carrier scooped them both up and stuffed Hans under one arm and Greta under the other like they were two loaves of French bread.

The mail carrier deposited them on the front seat of the mail truck. They rode a long way. Hans had his head out the window and slobbered all over the next day's mail. Greta slithered to the floor and gave the evil mail carrier the dirtiest looks she could come up with.

But, before they knew it, outside the mail truck window was the white picket fence and the big front porch and the windows down to the floor. Their mom was standing on the porch calling out, "Hans! Greta! Time to come in!"

The mail carrier opened the door and they ran home. They almost bruised their mom's ankles as they wagged their tails in happiness.

Later that night, over nice bowls of ice cream, Hans and Greta decided that maybe mail carriers weren't so bad after all!

Jackie
and
the
Beanpole

Jackie, an adorable Poodle, lived with her mother in the country with a cow named "Cow" (all the good cow names, like "Bessy" and "Elsie," were already taken).

One day, Jackie's mother gave Jackie

the bad news that they didn't have any more money to buy Milk Bones (which go really great with Cow's milk) and that they would have to sell Cow just to get by. So she sent Jackie out to sell Cow in the city.

Jackie was very sad as she led Cow down the road to the city. You see, Cow was Jackie's very best friend. When Jackie had problems, she could tell them to Cow and Cow would listen and quietly chew her cud instead of offering lots of useless advice.

Along the way, Jackie stopped at every fire hydrant to smell who'd been there before. As long as she was going to make this big trip to the city, she might as well stop and smell the hydrants, she thought.

When Jackie and Cow finally reached the city

limits, things started to go bad. As they tried to cross a busy street, they were almost hit by a car and the driver yelled at them, "Get out of the road, you animals!"

When they got back on the sidewalk, Cow decided she had to poop (it had been a very long walk). Unfortunately, a policeman was standing nearby writing tickets for people whose parking meters had expired. He came running up to Jackie and Cow.

"You can't let that beast soil the sidewalk. It's against the law. I'll have to take the cow in," he said. With that, the policeman grabbed the rope around Cow's neck and led her off down the street.

Jackie was nearly in tears, wondering what she'd tell her mother, wondering what would happen to

Cow, wondering if she could catch her tail if she really tried hard next time.

Then, suddenly, a very tall man appeared. He took one look at Jackie's sad face and he reached down to pick her up. "Now, now, don't whine. Are you lost?"

Jackie looked around. She was really way up high in the air. Higher than she'd ever been. This was fun. She turned and looked at the man who held her in his arms and licked him in the face.

"My name is Rudy," the tall man said. "I live right around the corner. Why don't we go to my apartment and I'll give you a bowl of milk and you'll feel much better."

Jackie started to cry again because the mention of milk made her think of Cow. Poor Cow spending the night in jail. She started to say something, but Rudy started walking really fast and she got dizzy.

When they got to Rudy's building, they got in an elevator (Jackie had never been in an elevator) and rode to the thirty-seventh floor. When she looked out the window, Jackie could look down on everyone in the city. This was heady stuff for a Poodle who'd never been out of the country.

As promised, Rudy poured Jackie a bowl of milk. And he poured it into a really nice china bowl, nicer than Jackie had ever seen. "I could get used to this," Jackie said to herself.

Jackie ran around the apartment and saw a nice big velvet couch, a big-screen TV, and a beautiful blue toilet.

Just then the phone rang. Rudy picked it up and

talked into it. Then he turned to Jackie and said, "I'm going to go out for a while. I'll be back and we'll see about getting you back home."

While Rudy was away, Jackie did some thinking. Her mom said there wasn't any money left. Cow was gone. Maybe the best thing to do was to stay with this nice rich man. That way her mom wouldn't have to worry about putting Milk Bones on the table for her every day.

So Jackie wriggled out of her dog collar and hid it under the couch.

Days went by. Rudy put an ad in the paper to see if anyone was missing a beautiful French Poodle. No one called. So he decided to keep her.

Jackie was very happy.

But, little by little, Jackie started to get sad and

homesick. There were no squirrels to chase up here in the air above the city. She had to wait until Rudy came home before she could go outside. Her little bladder was not used to waiting so long, so sometimes she made mistakes on the rug and the maid yelled at her. And every time she barked, the neighbors next door pounded on the wall and shouted, "Quiet in there, you mangy mutt!"

Jackie decided maybe she would be happier at home. Even without all the fancy toys Rudy had bought her to make her feel wanted. Even without the china dog dish. Even without the beautiful blue toilet.

So that day Jackie retrieved her collar from under the couch and wriggled back into it. When Rudy came in, he saw her wearing it and said, "Now where did that come from?" He immediately picked up the phone and called her mom.

Jackie's mom came to Rudy's apartment right away. She rushed up to Jackie and grabbed her in her arms. "Jackie, Jackie, I was so worried about you. I thought you had run away."

Jackie was very sorry she had made her mom worry. She understood that she had been wrong about things being better if she weren't at home. Her mom cared more about Jackie than having enough money. Jackie cried and cried.

Through her tears, Jackie explained to her mom about Cow. Unfortunately, although her mom had made a little money selling homemade cookies shaped like fire hydrants, it wouldn't be enough to spring Cow from jail.

Just then, Rudy jumped up and said, "I'll pay to get her out of jail. It's the least I can do."

So Jackie, her mom, and Cow all returned to their quiet little house in the country. Most people thought they were poor, but they were very, very rich.

Goldilocks
and *the*
Three Cats

*O*nce upon a time there were three
cats—Papa Cat, a very big black cat with
a white patch over his eye, Mama Cat, a
medium-sized tabby cat with orange stripes,
and Baby Cat, a very little cat with no tail.

Baby Cat was not actually Papa and

Mama's baby. They were not related at all. Baby Cat had just showed up at their door one day and wouldn't go away. You know how cats are.

The Cat family lived in a small house in the forest. If you want to know the truth, Papa Cat had lived in the big city, but when he heard his people talking about getting him declawed, he grabbed Mama Cat and they hightailed it as far away as they could. This is where they ended up.

In the house, there were three chairs—a huge barcalounger for Papa Cat (who liked to watch fishing while taking a catnap), a medium-sized swivel chair for Mama Cat (who liked to unravel sweaters and play with the yarn), and a tiny rocking chair for Baby Cat (who liked to pretend she was a cat on the high seas, rocking back and forth). All of the chairs were ripped to shreds because the Cats sharpened their nails on them every day.

Upstairs there were three beds—well, by now you know the sizes and who they belonged to. You, after all, are a dog and you catch on quick.

One morning, Mama Cat made some cat chow for breakfast. She filled three bowls (large, medium, and small . . . you know the drill) and put them on the table. Now we all know that cats aren't supposed eat on the table, but cats will be cats.

She also poured a big bowl of milk.

But for some reason known only to cats, Papa Cat, Mama Cat, and Baby Cat decided to go out and lie in the sun in a nearby meadow instead of eating their breakfast. Cats often just wander off to take a nap without finishing what they started.

This is why cats make lousy secretaries.

As the Cats were napping peacefully nearby, a Cocker Spaniel named Goldilocks was taking a walk through the woods to see what new smells there were to be smelled.

She came to the Cats' house. "I wonder who lives there," thought Goldilocks, who always was a little too curious for her own good. In fact in this way she was more like a cat than a dog.

The door was open so she went in to take a sniff around.

The first thing she noticed was the smell. There were three cat boxes right next to the door. For once in her life, Goldilocks was sorry she had such a good nose. She pushed the cat boxes into a closet and closed the door. "That's better."

Then Goldilocks saw the three chairs. She was appalled by the damage. If she treated the furniture like that at home, her people would make her take obedience lessons again.

Suddenly, the bowls on the table caught Goldilocks's eye. "You know, I am pretty hungry," she thought to herself. "That was kind of a long walk." After several attempts, she managed to jump up on a kitchen chair and put her paws on the table.

She sniffed the big bowl. "Yuck, cat food!" And so on with the other two bowls until she reached the bowl of milk. "Now we're talking," Goldilocks said, and then she drank the whole bowl.

But, as everyone knows, milk contains trypto-phan, which makes dogs and people sleepy. So, Goldilocks got very sleepy.

She went outside to pee on a bush and then came back inside for a nap. Upstairs she found the three beds. She tried to jump on the big one but it was too high. The middle-sized bed was covered with cat hair and made her sneeze.

But the littlest bed was a lot like her own bed at home. So Goldilocks lay down and went to sleep.

Meanwhile, the Cats were each stretching and yawning out in the meadow. Finally, they decided to go back home and have their breakfast.

The moment they stepped into the house, they knew someone had been there. Papa Cat said, "Someone's moved the litter boxes." Mama Cat said "Someone drank all the milk." Then she found a long curly blond hair on the table and looked over at Papa Cat and said "I don't suppose you can explain this?"

But just as Papa Cat began to stammer out a reply, Baby Cat, who was by now all the way upstairs in the bedroom, said, "Someone's sleeping in my bed!"

Mama Cat gave Papa Cat a look that sent shivers up his spine. They both ran to the bedroom.

When they got there they saw that the intruder was a dog. Papa Cat was very relieved. Mama Cat couldn't blame him this time.

Goldilocks awoke from her nap, opened her eyes and saw the three cats staring at her. She was very afraid. After all, the only cat Goldilocks had ever really gotten close to had scratched her nose.

Papa Cat sounded angry when he asked, "What are you doing in our house?" Mama Cat sounded really annoyed when she added, "And why did you drink all our milk?" But Baby Cat looked at Goldilocks and begged, "Can we keep her? Please?"

Well, to make a long story short (we know you have important things to do, like nap on the couch and bark at the birds), Goldilocks became good friends with the Cat family. And whenever she needed to get away from the pressures of big-city living, Goldilocks was welcome to visit (as long as she knocked first and paid for any milk she drank).

Which just goes to show you, no matter how different we are, we can still be friends.

Red, Riding to the Dog Show

*T*his is the story about Red, a beautiful Irish Setter who lived with two mixed breeds named Louie and Vinny, and three cats named Larry, Curly, and Moe, and some people whose names she could never remember.

Red was pretty happy with her life. Every day she got to run in the big backyard and play with the other dogs. And every night one of the smallest people would brush her long beautiful coat until it shone like gold, well, not like gold because it was red. More like rubies, but not quite that red. Well, anyway, you get the idea.

One day, a woman came to visit Red's house. She took one look at Red and said, "That is the most beautiful dog I have ever seen!" Red could feel her head start to swell.

Well, before long, Red's people decided they should enter her in dog shows. Red kind of liked the idea—getting all dolled up and hitting the road . . . showing off her great beauty from coast to coast . . . winning ribbons and prizes.

There was lots to do to get ready. Red had to

stop playing with Louie and Vinny in the backyard because that would mat her coat. They got so mad that they wouldn't even talk to her anymore. They called her "Miss Stuck Up."

Red was no longer allowed to eat leftovers, either, only a very expensive, very tasteless dog food from a bag. "Yuck," she said quietly every night as Louie and Vinny and the cats ate fried chicken or spaghetti or tuna fish sandwiches.

And instead of a simple brushing every night, Red had to be shampooed, creme-rinsed, detangled, defleaed, and deliced (for all she knew). The people even sprayed some goop on her to make her coat even shinier. It smelled really bad, but whenever she tried to rub it off on the carpet, the people would tell her to stop.

Then they painted her nails. Sure, they painted them black, which was their natural color, but she felt like a tramp with nail polish on. To make sure the people were aware of her feelings about this, she absolutely refused to wear the bright green bows they bought to put in her hair.

But the worst part yet was when she saw the crate in the back of the station wagon. She thought she was going to get to ride all over the country with her head hanging out, her ears flapping in the wind, slobber smearing across the back windows. But, *no.* Apparently, putting her head out the window would ruin her new "look." So she rode quietly and miserably in her crate in back.

Finally, they got to the first dog show of Red's life. She had to admit that, despite all the misery, she was pretty proud to be there. And, she thought to herself, looking pretty good.

Someone called her number (No. 7, which was all wrong in Red's opinion. She was No. 1 and everyone could see that). She paraded proudly around the ring, then came to a halt in front of the judge's table.

The judge, a tired-looking woman with a tag on that read, JUDGE WOLF took one look at her and said, "My, what big teeth you have."

Red thought to herself, "The better to get my share of the leftovers," but then she remembered she wasn't allowed to have leftovers anymore. Judge Wolfe looked down at her notebook and scribbled something down. Red didn't like the looks of it (nor the smell).

Then the judge said, "My, what big ears you

have." And again she wrote something in her notebook. Red wanted to tell her that she could hear squirrels burying nuts two blocks away with her ears, but she was pretty sure the judge wouldn't care.

Then the judge grabbed her snout and stared right into her eyes and said, "My, what big eyes you have." Red was sure this must be a good thing because she could see birds flying way up in the sky. But, from the look on the judge's face, this was a bad thing too.

Finally, all the other Irish Setters came into the ring together. Red's self-esteem was suffering and she started looking around. "You know, her tail droops on the end," she thought to herself as she looked at No. 6. "And his color is all wrong," she muttered, referring to No. 3. As you know, misery loves company, and Red was pretty miserable.

Finally, the judge went to get the ribbons. Nervously, Red chewed on her lips with her big teeth. She shook her big ears. She looked straight ahead with her big eyes.

When all the ribbons had been handed out, Red had one. A yellow ribbon. Sixth place. Out of seven.

Red's tail dragged. Her ears hung low. Her eyes blinked back tears. The humiliation of it all. She was not the most beautiful dog on earth. She wasn't even the most beautiful dog in the ring. She was nothing.

But then a wonderful thing happened. When Red got to the car, she noticed the crate wasn't there. It had been sold to a German Shepherd's people.

Red was invited to ride in the front seat. With

her head out the window. And when they got home they took the polish off her nails and threw the green ribbons away.

And that night, as the smallest person was combing her hair, she said to Red, "You'll always be the most beautiful dog in the world to me!" And then, noticing that Louie and Vinny looked depressed, the girl said, "One of the three most beautiful dogs— Louie and Vinny are the other two."

And they all lived happily every after. Red never went to another dog show. She played in the yard every day with Louie and Vinny. And, even though she still thought she was beautiful, Red thought everyone else was too—in their own way.

Snow White and the Seven Chihuahuas

*N*ot so long ago, a really smart German Shepherd named Snow White was training to become a guide dog for the blind.

Snow was very proud of himself (yes, that's right, Snow White was a boy dog, although he had been fixed when he was still a puppy). He was proud of himself because back in obedience school his teachers had said he would never get very far.

As it turns out, he was just not very good at taking tests and was a really smart dog after all. He showed them!

Across town lived another German Shepherd named Queenie who thought she was the smartest dog in the world. Every day she'd look into her dog bowl (which was so shiny Queenie could see herself in it) and ask, "Dog food bowl on the floor, who's the smartest dog in Poughkeepsie?" (Queenie was not much of a poet.)

And every day, her dog food dish would reply, "You, Queenie, are a genius. There's not another dog in the entire state who could match wits with you.

You'd probably have to go overseas just to find another dog with whom to have an intelligent conversation."

That was one talkative dog food dish.

But one day something unexpected happened. After Queenie finished her food and posed her nightly question to the bowl, this is the answer she got: "Well, I hate to tell you this, especially since your teeth are so sharp and you could tear me to pieces, but word on the street is that there's a dog named White, Snow White, working at training to become a guide dog for the blind and he's the smartest dog of all. We kind of missed him before because he tested so poorly . . ."

Queenie didn't hear the rest because she had run out of the house in a fit of anger.

But Queenie was not one to just take bad news pleasantly. Instead she rounded up five of the meanest dogs in the neighborhood (they had all been abused as children and, although they were in therapy, they were still pretty vicious). She told them to go chase Snow White out of town.

Which is exactly what they did. Well, kind of.

You see, the mean dogs found Snow White helping a man with a blindfold on, and despite their tendency to fight first and ask questions second, they were very much impressed by Snow White's skills and dedication. So, instead of beating him up and running him out of town, they simply scent-marked all his spots and told him he'd better hide out for a few days.

Snow White decided he'd better follow their

advice, so, after writing a grammatically correct and prosaically perfect note to the head of the guide dog school, he decided to go hide out in the country with his friend Chester.

He ran through the woods for hours and finally came to the house he was looking for. Even though it had been over a year since he'd been there, he was sure it was the right place because he smelled the curb. Besides, the mailbox read, CHESTER AND HIS CHA-CHA BAND.

"So, it's true," thought Snow White, "Chester is doing the music gig. Good for him."

Snow White knocked but no one answered. He tried to stick his head in the the doggie door, but only his snout would fit. For, you see, Chester and all his band members were Chihuahuas.

So Snow White went around back. Chester always used to leave the back door unlocked when he lived in the city. And, sure enough, the door was open. Snow White went in.

The place was a real mess. There were soiled newspapers in one corner. The carpet was full of fleas. Someone had left the top off the dog food container.

Snow White decided that he might as well clean up while he waited for Chester to return home. He also decided to repaint the living room and balance Chester's checkbook, which he had carelessly left lying on the table.

But all that flurry of activity left Snow White very tired, so he decided to catch a dog nap on the couch, which was almost big enough for him (and just a little too big for the entire seven-piece band and their girlfriends).

When Snow White awoke, Chester was singing a Caribbean calypso and the rest of the band were playing their instruments. It was a catchy tune, although Snow White actually preferred classic rock.

"Hey there, old man," Chester said when he noticed Snow White was awake. "Thanks for the work you did around here. I can't get these guys up off their lazy butts most of the time."

"No problem," responded Snow White. "So, you going to introduce me to your friends, or what?"

"Sure. This is Snoozy, he has narcolepsy. We never let him drive the van. And here's Whiney (don't get him started) and Perky. Perky's our PR guy. Over there's Beano (don't ask) and Dog (we're trying

to get him to change his name to something snazzier).
Last, but not least, this is Bruce. I'd stay out of his
way, he's a little moody sometimes.

For the next eight or nine minutes there was a
lot of tail-sniffing and other doggy greetings.

"So, Snow, buddy, what brings you out our
way?" Chester asked.

Snow White explained everything to the guys
and they seemed to be listening, although the TV
was on pretty loud and somebody kept changing
channels with the remote. "Do you think I could
hang with you for a while?"

"No problemo," said Beano. "Just be careful you
don't step on us, because that would probably hurt,"
added Whiney.

So, every day when Chester and the guys would

go off to do their Cha-Cha thing, Snow White would stay home and clean up. He also started on their taxes. He wanted to keep his intellectual skills polished.

Meanwhile, across town, Queenie finished a big bowl of dog food and once again asked, "Dog food dish on the floor, who's the smartest dog in Poughkeepsie?" (Not only was she bad at rhyming, she never learned.)

And, once again, the dog food bowl said, "Snow White." But then it added, "And I know where he is, if you'd like me to tell you. You want me to tell you, huh? What's in it for me? . . ."

Queenie shook the dog food bowl so hard it screamed out, "He's out in the country with Chester and His Cha-Cha Band."

She was so furious, Queenie went right down into the basement, found an old rawhide bone, and dipped it in rat poison. "I'll get that Snow White if it's the last thing I ever do," she barked.

In the middle of the night, Queenie made the long trip out to Chester's house and laid the bone on the front stoop. It had a note attached. TO SNOW WHITE: WE MISS YOU. YOUR FRIENDS AT THE GUIDE DOG SCHOOL.

The next morning after Chester and the guys had gone off to work (they were cutting their first CD), Snow White noticed the bone on the stoop. It was a really big bone. It looked delicious. And it had been over a week since Snow White had eaten anything that was nearly big enough.

So he started to gnaw on it right away, even

though his superior intellect should have questioned how anyone at the guide dog school could have found out where he was since he hadn't told them where he was going (for their own protection).

The poison took effect very quickly. When the guys got home, Snow White was lying motionless in the yard.

The guys were very sad. They dragged Snow White's lifeless body out by the big oak tree he liked to pee on and laid him there. (This was a lot of work for the guys, and Bruno developed a hernia about which he griped for years). They picked flowers and scattered them all around. They played sad ballads and cried.

While all of this was going on, a beautiful black Labrador and her person were walking down the sidewalk on the other side of the street. The Labrador's name was Lucy and she started to pull very hard at the leash, dragging her person behind her.

When they arrived at the memorial, Lucy asked Chester, "What happened?" Chester said he didn't know, but that Snow White appeared to be dead.

Lucy turned to her person and said, "Can you help him? He's so beautiful, lying there so peacefully." Then she turned to the boys and said, "My person is a vet. Maybe it's not too late."

Lucy's person kneeled down beside Snow White. He listened to Snow White's chest and said, "I hear a faint heartbeat, but he's not breathing." The vet put his mouth on Snow White's and started administering CPR. "One, two, three, four," he counted.

Soon Snow White started to breathe on his own. Chester and the band were so excited they started playing joyful songs, but they were so excited they weren't in sync. (It's a good thing the record producers didn't hear them!)

Lucy was very happy because she thought Snow White was beautiful. Snow White was happy because, well, being alive is always better than being dead.

In the end, Snow White and Lucy got married. Snow White taught Lucy how to be a guide dog for the blind and they worked side by side every day for a blind human couple. At night they lived with the vet, who was a really nice man.

And what happened to Queenie? Well, she continued to fret about who was the smartest dog of all and practically drove herself insane. And she never learned about love—which just goes to show she wasn't really that smart after all.

CinderDane

Once upon a time there was a Great Dane named CinderDane. Her coat was blue-black, the color of charcoal. She was so dark that even though she was almost as tall as a horse, at night she could hide outside and no one would see her.

And although she was big and smart and her coat was beautiful, CinderDane had really low self-esteem.

For, you see, she lived with three small dogs— Beagle Bob, Tom Terrier, and New Yorkie—who were always running around her legs and causing her to trip. Many times behind her back they would laugh at her and call her "the Klutz." They never did this to her face becasue they were afraid of her; after all, she could probably eat them for breakfast if she had a mind to.

But CinderDane was a sweetheart. A pussycat, really. She wouldn't hurt a flea intentionally (and she had plenty of them!).

In her whole life CinderDane had never met a dog nearly as big as she was. There was Dominick, the Dalmation who lived three houses down, but even he could walk under her tall legs.

CinderDane was certain she would never find anyone to love because she would never find anyone her own size.

Then, one day an invitation came in the mail to CinderDane's house:

<blockquote>
All Creatures Great & Small

Is having a holiday party

Tomorrow afternoon, 7 o'clock

Bring your toys and your people
</blockquote>

All Creatures Great & Small was the name of the kennel where CinderDane, Beagle Bob, Tom Terrier, and New Yorkie would stay when their people had to go away. It was a pretty nice place and CinderDane always had fun there, even though, as usual, she was always the biggest dog and often the other dogs yelped and screeched when she accidentally stepped on them (she really couldn't see them all the way down there).

A party invitation might have been exactly what CinderDane needed to help cheer her up. Unfortunately, however, earlier that day she had been to the vet for her regular checkup and one of the technicians had said, "Whoa, look at the size of that dog!" And he didn't mean it as a compliment.

So, CinderDane was really down in the dumps that day and just lay in the middle of the living room floor staring vacantly into space.

Beagle Bob, Tom Terrier, and New Yorkie, on the

other hand, were very excited about the party. So excited, in fact, that Tom Terrier left a little puddle on the floor. (Another thing CinderDane couldn't do because she would flood the whole house!)

They spent all morning trying to decide what to wear. Beagle Bob chose his blue sweater with the red buttons. Tom Terrier opted for his Hawaiian print shirt, visor, and sunglasses. New Yorkie, always the height of fashion, chose a T-shirt that looked like a tuxedo, with a red bow tie.

And off they went, leaving CinderDane sleeping on the rug.

CinderDane started to dream. She dreamed her fairy godmother showed up and offered to help her get ready for the party. "I'm here to grant your wish," said the fairy godmother.

"You mean you can make me smaller?" asked CinderDane in her dream.

"If that's what you really want," replied fairy godmother, "but I wouldn't advise it. You're a beautiful dog just like you are. I happen to like big dogs."

But CinderDane was adamant. She wasn't going to the party unless she was small enough to play with the other dogs without hurting them. She wanted to fit through a dog door, jump on the sofa without breaking it, and eat dog bones that didn't come from dinosaurs.

With a "1, 2, 3 . . . Poof," fairy godmother shrank CinderDane. She was the size of a Sheltie, only she still looked like a Great Dane.

"Wonderful," thought CinderDane in her dream.

And, as usually happens in dreams, the next thing she knew she was at the party. All the other dogs were having Milk Bones and ice cream and playing "Sniff the Tail on the Donkey."

When CinderDane walked in the room, no one noticed her. She said hello to Beagle Bob, Tom Terrier, and New Yorkie, but they didn't seem to know she was there. So she climbed up on top of a chair and started to bark, trying to get everyone's attention to show off her "new look." But no one noticed.

CinderDane started to get frustrated. Then she became sad. Finally, she ended up barking out for her fairy godmother, "I want to be a big dog again. I want to be a big dog again."

Then she woke up.

CinderDane stood up and looked at herself in the mirror. She decided maybe being the biggest dog wasn't all that bad. After all, everyone always noticed her when she was in the room.

So, she decided to go to the party.

CinderDane trotted down the street, taking her big dog steps and proudly holding her head up as she greeted everyone along the way. This time when people pointed and stared, she was happy.

When CinderDane arrived at the party, all the dogs were playing, just like in her dream. But when she walked in, everyone barked hello (and, well, let's face it, a few barked to let her know she was standing on them.)

Then, something wonderful happened. In through the front door walked the most handsome dog CinderDane had ever laid eyes on—an Old English Sheepdog (CinderDane had seen pictures in a book) with beautiful long hair that fell across his eyes, giving him an air of mystery.

CinderDane walked right up to him and said, "Hi, my name is CinderDane. Welcome to the party."

"I'm Prince," said the handsome stranger, as he shook the hair out of his eyes. "And may I tell you that you are the most beautiful creature I have ever seen or smelled."

Well, like all stories, this one has to end. And this is the way it ends: CinderDane and Prince fell in love (it was love at first sight—well, second sight for Prince because his hair was in his eyes the first time).

And, as they sat in front of a fire in the fireplace,

CinderDane thought to herself, "I guess there is someone for everyone. You're right, fairy godmother, I am happy being a big dog."

Princess
and
Peabody

There once was a Basset Hound named Princess. She was from Georgia and when she barked, she had a sweet southern accent.

"Bark, y'all," she'd bark at the mail carrier. "Howdy, bark bark" she'd bark when her person returned from work.

Princess was a very spoiled dog. She had her own brass bed with a handmade quilt. She ate dinner out of a lovely crystal bowl. She had sweaters and T-shirts and rain ponchos and evening wear . . . and jewelry, lots and lots of jewelry.

She also had lots of toys. Her favorites were her squeaky toys. Every night, Princess would not go to sleep until she had piled up all her squeaky toys near her bed where she could keep an eye on them.

But, Princess was very lonely. Although she lived with a very nice person, she spent most of the day home alone. And there were no dogs around for her to play with. Playing with her toys by herself every day got very boring.

So one day she decided to put an ad in *DogFancy*. This is what she wrote:

FBH (female Basset Hound), smart, intelligent, well-off, good sense of humor. I enjoy short walks on the beach, Lassie movies, and chewing Italian leather shoes. Searching for companion who enjoys the same. No smoking, no drugs, no fleas. Let me be your Southern Princess.

Pretty soon the mail carrier dropped a letter through the slot in the front door of Princess's house. "Bark, bark. Ya'll come back now," she said.

She ripped the envelope open with her nails (they were really long because Princess really hated getting her nails done and Princess almost always got her way.)

The letter said:

"Dear Southern Princess—I would love to meet you. You sound like a wonderful girl and maybe we could have fun together. Why don't you call me at 555-RUFF? Yours, Peabody.

Princess was very excited. She called Peabody's number right away.

They talked for a while and agreed they would meet at Princess's house the next day at 10:00 A.M.

That night, Princess could hardly sleep, she was so excited. She tossed and she turned all night long. She was finally going to have a friend to play with. She really hoped everything worked out.

The next day at 10:25 A.M., a Corgi showed up at the front door. It was Peabody and he was twenty-five minutes late. Princess was a little miffed. She wasn't used to being kept waiting.

But she opened the door, smiled, and said, "Come on in and make yourself at home. Could I git ya'll some iced tea?"

"That sounds real nice," Peabody said as he

made three circles and laid down on the floor. "I really like your accent," he added.

"Thanks," Princess said as she went into the kitchen to get the tea. Suddenly, she heard a noise from the living room. She rushed out to find that Peabody had broken her crysal water dish.

"Oh, my gosh, how did y'all happen to do that?" she asked as politely as she could manage.

"I'm really sorry. I wasn't looking where I was going and I guess I just knocked it into the wall. I apologize—it was a lovely bowl."

"Handblown crystal," Princess muttered under her doggy breath. "Been in the family for twehnny dog years."

Princess was really upset, but being a southern lady, she smiled her biggest Basset Hound smile and served the iced tea.

Peabody drank his tea quickly. Then he looked over at the handmade quilt on her bed and asked, "Would you mind if I used that quilt? The iced tea has made me quite cold."

Princess hesitated. It was her quilt. No one else had ever used it. But, she must be polite, so she dragged the quilt over to the couch and Peabody buried himself under it.

Princess noticed that Peabody was shedding all over the quilt. Trying to be polite, she took the glasses back to the kitchen. Then she returned.

"So, whut is it you do for a livin'?" Princess asked.

"I'm a hearing dog. I let people who can't hear know when the phone's ringing or there's a knock on the door."

"Oh, how nice." Princess had to be impressed.

After all, this showed that Peabody had a good heart.

"And you?" asked Peabody.

"Oh, ah guahd the house. Nobuddy gits in this house without me sayin' so."

They talked for fifteen more minutes and then Peabody asked, "Would you mind if I played with some of your squeaky toys? I don't have any of my own at home."

"Well, do ya think that would be, uh, sanitary?" Princess whined. She really did not want him putting his mouth on *her* toys.

"Oh, that's no problem. You know they say that dogs' mouths are very clean. Besides, I brush every night."

Princess tried another tack. "Don't ya think it's a little eahly in our . . . uh . . . relationship to share ouh things?"

Peabody was hurt. "I wasn't talking about moving in or anything. I just wanted to toss a few balls around. Jeez, you certainly are selfish. Maybe I should go."

Princess had second thoughts. "All right, maybe it'd be okay. Ah didn't mean anythin' by it . . ." She went over and searched through her pile until she found her least favorite toy. She presented it to Peabody royally. "He-ah, how about this one?"

Peabody seemed pleased and he played for a while. Princess watched him to make sure he didn't ruin the squeaker.

Then Peabody got very tired. "Do you suppose I could take a short nap?" he asked. Princess didn't see any problem with that.

But then Peabody went over and laid down on

her brass bed. She could just imagine all the long Corgi hairs she'd have to brush out. This was just too much for her.

"Ah'm sorry, Peabody. This just doesn't seem to be workin' out. You'll have to go now."

So, Peabody left. And Princess had the whole house to herself. Again.

Days went by.

Princess started thinking about how much fun it was drinking tea with Peabody. And talking to him. And watching him play with her toys.

Maybe she'd been a little selfish, after all he was a guest in her home. And he was fun to be around.

So Princess swallowed her pride and called Peabody. Here's what she said: "Peabody, ah'm sorry about the other day. Sometimes I forgit and I think things are important. But I really know they're not. Things are not important. Friends are important. If you'll be my friend, I promise neveh to be stingy agin."

After that Peabody and Princess became very best friends. They shared her things and she didn't mind at all. Well, she minded a little bit, but she got over it.

Nursery Rhymes

Peter, Peter

Peter, Peter, just got paid
Still didn't get his little dog spayed.
Now there's ten puppies in his bed
If only he had used his head.

🦴   🦴   🦴   🦴

Little Miss Muffin

Little Miss Muffin
Her hair all a-fluffin'
Was eating her kibbles and bits
Along came a spider
And sat down beside her
And Muffin also ate it

Humpty Dumpty

Humpty Dumpty peed on a wall
Humpty Dumpty was very tall
And all the king's Corgis and all the king's Pugs
Had to settle for peeing on the rugs.

Jack and Jill

Jack and Jill went up the hill
To fetch a ball and stick
Jack laid down upon the ground
And checked for fleas and ticks.

Three Small Dogs

Three small dogs
Three small dogs
Hear how they bark
Hear how they bark
They barked all day and they barked all night
They kept away trouble with all their might
Three small dogs.

Hickory Dickory Dog

Hickory Dickory Dog
The mutt scratched in the fog
The fog rolled out
He rubbed his snout
Hickory Dickory Dog.

Angel Dogs

Not very long ago in a part of the world that has mountains and oceans and lots of rain, lived two Dachshunds named Copper and Slate.

They lived with their mother and father. Well, not their real mother and father.

Because, you see, Copper and Slate were adopted when they were just puppies. But their adopted mom and dad loved them just as much as if they had been their own children.

Copper and Slate were twelve years old, which is not as young as they used to be, but not old either. And Mom got really mad at people when they looked at the gray hairs on Copper and Slate's muzzles and said, "How old are they?" Because to her they would always be her puppies.

And every day of every year of their life, Mom had been sure of one thing—Copper and Slate were angel dogs.

At first, Dad didn't believe it. After all, they had never saved anyone from a burning building. And they were too short to help guide people who couldn't see. And sometimes, they acted like devils, especially when they peed on the living room carpet because they thought it was too cold outside.

But Mom knew. She knew you didn't have to be a hero to be an angel dog. She knew you could even behave like a devil sometimes and still be an angel dog.

She knew that Copper, the red Dachshund, was an angel dog because he:

Purred when she rubbed his ears (yes, dogs do purr!)

Saved all his kisses for Mom and Dad and never kissed anyone else

Snored loudly when he slept

Refused to get up in the mornings until he had had all the love he deserved

Stood at his dog bowl and said as clear as day, "I know you think I've had enough food, but I disagree"

Outsmarted his brother when they played chase

Barked at everything just in case it was important

Had the three most precious and valuable diamonds in the world right there on his chest

Had a tail that looked like someone had dipped it in white paint

Had paws that smelled like popcorn

Could say more with one look than most people could say in their whole lives

Never met a trash can he didn't want to dump over.

Slate, the black-and-tan Dachshund, was an angel dog for completely different reasons, including because he :

Wagged his tail so hard when Mom and Dad came home that he nearly fell down

Despite years of failing, still believed in his heart that he could catch a squirrel

Wouldn't go to sleep at night unless he was curled under his mom's arm

Insisted on having his teeth brushed before going to bed at night

Kept Mom company when she worked on the computer by lying on the loveseat and watching her

Knew when anyone was getting food out of the refrigerator no matter how quiet they were about it

Had a muzzle that smelled like a field of flowers

Decided when it was time to stop a walk by sitting down in the middle of the road and refusing to budge

Played with stuffed animals, tossing them over his head and catching them in the air

Wouldn't eat his dinner until he threw his dog dish all around the kitchen like a big hockey puck.

Now, these may not sound like the things you think of when you think of angels. But Mom knew that every morning, Copper and Slate made her happy to wake up and happy to greet the day. And every day, she and Dad had fun and laughter and tears because of Copper and Slate.

And that's what angels do, isn't it?

So, finally, Dad agreed. In fact, he bought Copper and Slate haloes and wings from the pet store. He put them on and took their pictures. Of course, they rubbed and rolled and tried to get them off.

But they didn't fool Mom and Dad. They knew Copper and Slate were angels.

Just like you know your dog is an angel too.